Rumors of Ecstasy...
Rumors of Death

Grace Butcher

the
Barnwood Press
RIVER HOUSE
R.R. 2 Box 11C Daleville, Indiana 47334

The author is grateful for permission to reprint poems which first appeared in the following publications: *South and West:* "Nevertheless" 1971; *Polemic:* "Meditation Against The Grain" 1966; *Camels Coming:* "Split Second"; *Antioch Review:* "Sunbathing," "Results of The Polo Game"; *Hiram Poetry Review:* "Sky Diver," "Wife of The Moon Man Who Never Came Back," "The Young Wrestlers," "Rites by Now Familiar" 1970; *Frigate:* "No Visiting Hours"; *Free Lance:* "Training (in the woods)" 1966; *Dare:* "Therapy" 1967; *Trace:* "Some Sort of Death" 1968; *Jeopardy:* "Wild Rabbit" 1968; *Bitterroot:* "In Non Memoriam"; National Endowment for The Arts and Viking Press, *American Literary Anthology III; Runcible Spoon:* "Small Poem for A Short Sleep"; *International Who's Who in Poetry Anthology:* "Your Hand on My Hair Touches Deep Ghosts" 1971; *Poets on The Platform:* "Spring Sprang Sprung Song," "Aunt Dorothy," "In Fear of The Final Symphony" © 1970 The Ashland Poetry Press; *A Consort of Poets:* "Dog Show in Summer" © 1969 The Ashland Poetry Press.

This collection of poems by Grace Butcher was originally published in 1971 by The Ashland Poetry Press, Ashland College, Ohio.

Cover photograph by Larry Basar

CONTENTS

SKY DIVER 7

WIFE OF THE MOON MAN WHO NEVER CAME BACK 9

ON DRIVING BEHIND A SCHOOL BUS
  FOR MENTALLY RETARDED CHILDREN 10

TRAINING (IN THE WOODS) 11

TRAINING (ON THE TRACK) 13

SOME SORT OF DEATH 14

SUNBATHING POEM II 16

YOUNG WRESTLERS 18

RITES, BY NOW FAMILIAR 19

THERAPY 20

SPLIT SECOND 21

SMALL POEM FOR A SHORT SLEEP 22

NO VISITING HOURS 23

RESULTS OF THE POLO GAME 24

WILD RABBIT 26

MOBILITY TRAINING 29

ABSENCE MAKES THE HEART ETC. 30

THE WINTER NIGHT CHILDREN 32

AUNT DOROTHY 33

DOG SHOW IN SUMMER 35

GULL SONG AT LAND'S END 36

SPRING, SPRANG, SPRUNG SONG 38

A NARROW LIGHT BUT CERTAIN 39

IN HALF A DAY 40

HOUSE 41

ENGLISH 372 42

DECISION NOT TO COMMIT SUICIDE 44

NEVERTHELESS 45

MEDITATION AGAINST THE (G)RAIN 47

YOUR HAND ON MY HAIR TOUCHES DEEP GHOSTS 48

SEARCH 49

ASSIGNMENT 51

IN FEAR OF THE FINAL SYMPHONY 53

AN EXPLANATION OF THE AIR IMAGERY   55
    IN GRACE BUTCHER'S POETRY 55

IN NON MEMORIAM 57

JUST CHECKING 58

CYCLE SONG 59

A MATTER OF LIFE OR DEATH 61

For my sons, Dan and Claar

SKY DIVER

I. When you talk of falling,
   something in me closes,
   something opens.

   I would never
   no never

   never lie down upon the air
   in the terrible roar,
   the awful silence.

   But you allow me in,
   allow me to know
   the inside of your bones
   spread in flight . . .

   the hollow bones
   I inhabit long enough
   to see the great curve of horizon,
   how it fits the curve of our body

   until you blink and separate me
   from your bones,
   from the jarring of your blood,
   just before the earth reaches us.

II. And yet I brood upon

the beautiful fear
of falling deeply
through the possibly final air

wondering
for whose sake
it would be.

An ominous curiosity writhes:
rumors of ecstasy
haunt me like
rumors of death.

WIFE OF THE MOON MAN
WHO NEVER CAME BACK

Often when the moon is full
they have to give her something
to make her sleep.
She confuses "moon" with "mine"
and has been known
to run naked on the lawn
screaming his name
and singing children's songs.
The familiar face
terrifies her.

Certain nights
she opens the curtains,
the windows,
opens her thighs,
her darkest places.
His body, thin silver now,
pours into her with no warmth;
her fingers crawl like animals
to their dark hole.

Thrilled and horrified,
she breathes the rush of silver air
with lungs that grow thick.
It is a familiar feeling:
the dust falling on her open eyes,
shadows or someone screaming,
caught in the surge of gigantic tides.

9

ON DRIVING BEHIND A SCHOOL BUS FOR MENTALLY RETARDED CHILDREN

Full deep green
bloom-fallen spring
here outside,
for us.

They,
like winter-covered crocuses:
strange bright beauty
peeping through snow
that never melts—

(How quietly,
how quietly,
the bus.)

These flowers have no fragrance.
They move to an eerie wind
I cannot feel.
They rise, with petals fully opened,
from a twisted seed,
and neither grow
nor wither.

They will be taught
the colors of their names.

TRAINING (IN THE WOODS)

In these woods trees are always running
and clover drifting smells like pain
or sometimes very sweet and fast
even butterflies hang motionless
with the speed of the long green tunnel
rushing by especially to the end
which is always there and very golden.

Even the wind makes no difference
for the leaves fall when they will
and I have no feet only swirling leaves
golden below the knees a blur upward
to where woodchucks climb trees
did you know that
skunks stop all traffic on this road
where heat makes shadows of growing
even when all traffic is only
motionless on golden wheels
facing the miles on both sides
are just as long.

These woods are blurred
with very green breathing or sometimes
gray and brown and black breathing
in a cathedral running gothic trees
leaning over center aisle running
towards golden shining at the end of

sometimes very white breathing
and my feet are diamonds up to my ankles
to my knees to my thighs
and I disappear into blizzard
into blossoms where pain drifts up
on thin white wings or butterflies
and ripe fruit is golden when it falls
from running trees into my quiet hands.

TRAINING (ON THE TRACK)

Rainwings
pain-folded into night colors
running streaked into light and dark
cloud shadows chasing
bright fields of pain
shining wet and moving
hair touching softly
whipping into caress
of steady rhythm flowing
into black river of miles
and white lines of minutes
ticking of pain
in left right rhythm
climbing up above where
must stay here
stay here
stay here
no thoughts
sliding down into pain
only high higher climbing
into wind
where I become the wind
blowing
through bright fields of pain

SOME SORT OF DEATH

The heron
steps
    slowly

along the edge
of a certain dream

shattering two skies.

    Dark soft weeds
    move with the water

    dark with slime
    my hair still growing
    . . . even now.

The heron
walks
    across my eyes

His strange feet
change my face
        easily

    I need no form.
    This lake is enough.

I have two skies
although they break
and break
    where herons walk.

SUNBATHING POEM II

A small bug
greener than blaze of all
sun/moon iridescence
crawls on the hair
between my legs . . .

O, innocence of grass!
Jewels for the navel
and below.

One golden bee
worn just above
the left breast
more softly than sweat . . .

O, importance of quiet hills!
Heartbeat and dragonflies
probe the golden places.

Wrapped in warm clover wind
from shimmering hayfields
what is there left
for me to do but
close my eyes and die?

The sun carves
my body into caves

where bird song moves
like an underground stream.

Blind fish leap
as they feel
the coming of the light.
Everything is transparent
here.

(O, grass! O, quiet hills!)

YOUNG WRESTLERS

The beautiful boys curve and writhe,
gone inward behind their contorted masks.
The blind hands reach;
the legs hook, lock, lever
the gleaming bodies into hold,
out of hold. Escape. Riding time.
"Sink a half!" and the arm snakes
rapid with love around the neck.

One is left who will cry somewhere.
For the other, the air bends
in to him, hot with voices.
The walls reappear, the colors.
He is one body again,
lonely with joy.
Many sweet dreams will be based
on that ferocious touch.

RITES, BY NOW FAMILIAR

Spring is always uncertain;
otherwise, why the dancing,
why the sacrifice?
The knife is always obsidian,
the heart always still beating
held up for approval of the crowd.
What altar do you lay me down upon?
      . . . lay me down
        lay me down . . .
Love, I see you flowering
with my last eyes.

THERAPY

If I run long enough
I shall finally (like sand)
fall completely out of my head
into my body—

out of the glare and din of words
spoken aloud alone,
into an endless twilight
of coolness, of silent motion.

Through the sharp snow
my body darkens
like an explosion
of many birds.

SPLIT SECOND

How quickly death is gone.
There was a hummingbird
last week (or century ago)
that left just such an
empty space shimmering.

If death is anything,
it is (on wind of no words)
to be remembered thus:
terrible beauty, hovering
on no (dark) wings.

SMALL POEM FOR A SHORT SLEEP

Your face melts into dark
against my arm.
Strangely and somehow asleep,
I lean on one elbow
over you,
doze in the throbbing
of the slow pulse
at your throat.
It is our eyes asleep, Love,
that see into the deepest places,
and the beautiful quiet of your face
that opens me
to everything you are.

NO VISITING HOURS

When I am only there, and there,
through all colors of days
and the one-colored night,
think of my hair
(it will be the same)
on the pillow
(and once in the rain . . .)
and think of me younger
than what's-her-name
(the goddess of dawn)
but I won't have to cope
with the sun anymore
when I am (more or less)
gone.

RESULTS OF THE POLO GAME

The young boys forget about cars awhile,
saunter carefully casual to touch the lathered shoulder,
wait for the sweet monotony of walking the wet ones dry.
The ponies are tough and tired and friendly,
walk docilely for a hundred different hands
around the circuit of cities and grass.
The young girls love easily:
the sweet smell of the silken coats,
the immense deep moving of hidden muscle,
the fumbling soft lips, the fine boney heads.

But the boys are slower, reluctant to react
to the uncoiling of this unfamiliar love.
They carry the smell in their nostrils for hours,
stronger, stranger than perfume or gasoline.
In bed before sleep they walk the wet horses,
the heads still loom at their shoulders,
their fingers curve to the sweated leather.
There is the neck to touch, to arch with the arm;
comparisons to make: a thousand pounds of power
held by thin reins, the alien metal in the soft mouth.

The thighs ache to curve around this new body.
There is confusion about the meanings of love,
embarrassment at boundaries that will not stay put,
ambiguous language that always leads to lust:
the curves, the shine, the power, the deep sweet smell,

the capturing, taming, gentling; the moving together.
The girls already know. Their thighs are open.
It is a satisfactory substitute, this love.
The boys, in sleep, run a hand through the thick mane,
lay their faces against a shining shoulder, and decide.

WILD RABBIT

Lightning-brown oval

     splits

     white morning
     violet twilight grass.

My cat at the window

     is rigid with desire,

but if he feels her evil eye

     through the glass

     he only hunches
     the smooth hump of his back,

     lets it pass.

Stone-brown, earth-brown,
earthbound, fear-bounding:
fear felt, figured, fades,

He lingers at the best blades,

the chosen clover,

    careful hunger
    second in the silence,
    careless of the motionless,
    the birds, the blank wind.

But my son goes out, knows

from childhood there is one word:

    wild word,
    brown-sounding word

to speak in soft secret
to make him
let him
touch him.

But the word is loud-wrong,
long forgotten,

and the white tail tells no story.

Sudden and deep

    to the fields

he opens, folds.

There is only a slight tightening

    of sorrow.

My son says

    that the language is younger

    than anything he can remember,

but he thinks the rabbit

    will blaze brown-bright
    and fearful, fearless,
    here again tomorrow.

MOBILITY TRAINING

They were in the hotel parking lot:
the new blind boy
with a perpetual intake of breath
filling his uncertain mouth with questions,
and his perfect trainer
whose eyes had all the quick answers
of the world.

My eyes closed,
shutting me into thirty years
of touch and sound.
The shape of tears roared in my head
like a blinking train
at a remembered crossing,
carrying all pictures of people
away into a scream of night.

What if only hands
could light my invisible body,
and only my tightening skin
could echo brick walls?

I would try dark poems in the dust
with my cane; I would curse
and write words on top of words
over the brittle sound of paper,
angry at how my hands stumbled
and at the cumbersome shape
of the enormous dark pencil.

ABSENCE MAKES THE HEART ETC.

So maybe my mother
who died
       now
a flower is

I only remember
her or was it Grandma
genes and chromosomes
a tangle of both
and all three of us
planted
       we just
looked for empty
spaces and put things
there
       no matter how big
they might grow
someday
       No plan
but daffodils shock
the shadows
       the small
tree grows
       I
cannot transplant it
too tangled
       yes

in sky
        It would
pull pieces out

(Maybe my mother
would look down
through the holes
tell me something
ridiculous like
how are you)

            I wish
the flowers could
see her.

THE WINTER NIGHT CHILDREN

When the boys, behind their vague masks of breath,
give chase to all imagined winter ghosts,
they are shadows on the white spread of night,
bodiless, swooping across the dry cold.
I watch them circle the buildings, bushes—
the gang, navigating like bats somehow,
flit in and out shrieking the lack of moon.
They are all the same dark against the snow;
I cannot even tell which ones are mine.
Like some race existing before the sun,
living on white things dug out from black ice,
they sense their transformation, skillfully
feel their way across dark crystals of air.
They have no fear of the blackened angel
someone has made by falling in the snow;
no one has told them: be afraid or cold.
In infinite, unseen variations,
They have no need of faces until morning.

AUNT DOROTHY

I remember the burdock burrs
when they were purple with flowering,
and soft.
I brought them to my aunt
who sat on the end of the slide
in the playground by the country school.
We made baskets and balls and nests
and incredible purple-green things,
prickly and soft,
where the swings and rings and trapeze were,
and the teeter-totter strange-looming
out of the high grass.

Later burrs were brown and harsh
and hooked the skin,
but these were magic, flower-like,
under our gentle handling.

I still see the swings and all,
dark and fragile with memory
in the heat-filled field
against the sky,
and my aunt, who somehow made sculptures
out of flowers, out of weeds.

I think of her now like her garden was
in the afternoons on the farm:

poppies I remember most, then hollyhocks,
and bright vague masses of color and love.

She gave me serenity in the sun
and wild nests of purple-green
for imaginary birds
that must have been beautiful . . .
gentle things to write about years later.

She was better
than almost anybody.

DOG SHOW IN SUMMER

The dogs lie flat and exotic as rugs
in the heat under the tent.
    The men talk of stud fees and bitches,
    the women of litters and silver.
Childish fingers move the silken hair about,
search for a reality:
    in all that gleam of sable,
    in all that astonishing gold,
    where is the wet nose,
    the profered paw?

In the ring
    the squeaky rubber toy is tossed
    to lift the ears
    and brighten the eyes.
    The slobber is wiped away;
    the paws are planted
    in the flamboyant grass.
Be like a stone, dear doggy.
    Never mind the children
    who take part of you home
    in good faith on the bottoms
    of their shoes, wipe their feet
    when told, and ask how come
    nobody wagged his tail?

GULL SONG AT LAND'S END

The tanker Torrey Canyon, wrecked on
Seven Stones Reef, March 18, 1967,
carried 120,000 tons of oil. Most of it
washed ashore on the Cornwall Coast.

The people gather,
sorrowful in the sweet smoke.
They cannot wash the water
or burn the ocean clean.
They cannot undo the small deaths
a thousand times, or even once.

The oil burns hot and high;
my head is higher than the air.
I pour myself through space;
my days are burning.
Excitement shrieks inside my head
like screams of other birds.

Trembling, I swim through air
of endless thick days.
I would come down
to dawn-cold ocean,
but the oil burns
the dreams of night away.

I would come down
but the water heaves,

smashes the rocks black
for the rest of my forever;
and I am stretched too thin
across the air.

The people gather to watch
the ocean burn. None look up
at my last whiteness.
I am too high, too small,
too far away,
sick with the sweet air.

SPRING, SPRANG, SPRUNG SONG

Roar tight the wrapped wind
long around my strong house;
    a melting happens here.
Under the hunger my easy head
lifts wind's laughter out
    to spread the hanging hair.

No less than buds in bright white
breathed by silence black to green,
    the air swarms with sun.
Other perfumes than the pine
break the earth to make the heart
    hurt, the nerves sing.

Now lie lay lain leaping
swollen snow and swelling words
    to fierce mouths, eyes;
touch thunders moldy leaves
and strips the sky for opening.
    Washed, and wished, we rise.

A NARROW LIGHT BUT CERTAIN

So I shall practice sorrow in my love,
stand in thin sun from old windows and grieve:
inevitability of the grave,
monotony of death, partitioned lives.

So I shall quietly and whitely doze,
and you (if you have learned me properly)
will crave this length of winter, hate the lies
of necessary spring and better days.

So we shall wonder little, blink our eyes
at repetitions of the sun and moon;
a briefer death than death I take for mine,
and you are content in your frozen place.

A narrow light, but certain: we can share
the cliffs of winter, marvelous and sheer.

IN HALF A DAY

From suicide to clown
with sad eyes
(painted). My brain
is many colors, vague,
like massed flowers:
total spectrum of petals,
beginning with black.

I wear my costume inside
like blood and bones,
keep graphs of my ups and downs,
discover people laugh more
at my falls than at my flying.
The moral of this story is:
sad eyes need also tears.

HOUSE

I feel the stiff mechanisms of the earth
turn you closer;
it is I who stay here
in the serene century
of this house.

Stone roots,
deeper than flowers or orchard,
will reach like certain snakes for your legs.
I can walk a ways to meet you;
do not look down
to see my stone feet.

There are no roots
in all your avenues of wind:
have you not been lonely?
Spring and summer come here
with all the certainty
of a stone warm in the sun.
Fall has blood enough to nourish everything,
and in the winter we too sleep.

I feel the stone fibers
moving in the ground.
Kiss me and come in:
this house is held here
no matter how the rest of the world
grinds and turns.

ENGLISH 372

(Dedicated to the guy who sat next to me
because he was there when I needed him.)

My tongue
        a desert
of nothing quite said.

Sandstorm
        of words
from directly ahead
torment
for eyes or mouth kept open
with no camel
        to crouch behind.

Staggered
        by the glare
of an immovable sun
I seek the shade
        of my own shadow
and lie slowly down
one hand feebly raised . . .
into which is put
        O Miracle! O Friend!
a Lifesaver
        spearmint mirage

        clean green leaves

circle
cool pool of taste

Oasis
blossoms
and
a white racing camel
carries me
          laughing
away.

DECISION NOT TO COMMIT SUICIDE

I can no longer ignore the silver death
of dandelions: more beautiful
than any dying I could do.
Brown alive and into summer
we are (you and I) here—there.
It is the same sun.
Death is far small silver
in the huge air.

NEVERTHELESS

I had not intended

but I wish us love
in sun, in bright light
with open eyes, open doors.

I wish us in the woods,
in the hayfields, in any meadow
with no eyes open
but our own
and if flowers can see . . .

I had not intended

but I want to know
how the sun finds its way
through your thick hair
and I would follow
its path with my fingers.

And I want you to know
how my body is sleek
in its summer skin
and I want to touch you awake
hot with sleep in the naked grass

and I wish . . .

but I had not intended.

and I want . . .
(but I had not intended.)

MEDITATION AGAINST THE (G)RAIN

Up the rain
going up the rain to find
    the Source of Everything
hard work, this!
like up a waterfall
or impaled on the arrow of a one way street
or rubbing the cat's fur the wrong way
    stop!
this is the hard way to do it
like a splinter under a fingernail
or chalk screech on a blackboard
teeth clenched
shuddering
      stop!
rain slicing me into nervous pieces
why did I try to go this way?
slide down the rain
    ah!
better
cooler
find another way
or
    yes!
wait for the rainbow
which has no splinters
climb smoothly
laughing at my
    redorangeyellowgreenblueviolet feet.

YOUR HAND ON MY HAIR
TOUCHES DEEP GHOSTS

It's something old in the gesture, I guess,
from beyond vague boundaries I can't name.
Maybe my father once, in some dead noon,
loved me for a moment and touched me thus.
Or my grandfather with dead ears, at whom
I screamed my loud love: he knew how to touch
young things, young animals.

                         I have wept, reached
often enough for gone and ghostly hands,
even too far: under slow, quiet grass
into dead dimensions where there are none
with flesh to break my silent flesh.

                            At home
with searching, I am loathe to end the search;
yet something about your hands is the same
as someone's. Touch me; all death will end soon.

SEARCH

(to my mother, who is dead)

Were her years of me only empty rooms
with bright-colored wallpaper?
Where was she in all that thickness of space?
Doors cut through the flowers
led only to other empty rooms
where air swirled with her passing.

Wind of some faint far love
(where *was* that universe?)
blows fine dust over separate hands
that touched once.

Anger was good.
It was always a miscalculation,
an unexpected meeting in vague doorways.
The collisions crumbled walls
that cried out in my voice
and left real wounds for bloody kissing.
(O suck these wounds—
there is no poison here!)

Death didn't work.
I blunder now through galaxies of empty rooms,
searching through bright, still flowers
with no doorways.

Her universe moves always away,

the colors less bright in the distance.

Awkward, and hurrying too much,

I look through the wrong end of the telescope.

Only our eyes touch.

We look hunger through the stars.

ASSIGNMENT

Hey Mom!
(God said
let there be)
Gimme some
Flour & Water
(let the waters be)
I gotta Make
(let the dry land)
The World
It's due
Next week
(and there was evening)
Whatta mess
It's not even round
(and there was morning)
& it smells funny
Hey, could ya gimme
them Bride 'n Groom dolls
from your old cake
(male and female
he created)
They're kinda big
but I'll stick
their feet in good
(you are dust)
Wait'll the kids
(behold)

I bet Nobody Else
thought about
Making
(It was Very Good)
a World.

IN FEAR OF THE FINAL SYMPHONY

O wondrous young man
sleeping under my hair,
I have watched you too long
and grown stupid with love.
I turn into a frog
at first morning light.
I should have told you,
and I care—no matter what
I might have said—I care.

Anxiety gathers:
a great and terrible song
in my bulging throat.
The night grows brittle
and breaks apart. I feel
the drift of black flakes
settle on my face, and
something much like tears.
I feel the changing start.

Wake and rise, now, before day;
buckle on your shining skin
while I still am beautiful.
You may return in a hundred years—
(that's what I was told to say.)
Let the moonlight glaze your sight
and seal my present image in,

or your nightmares will begin
with the opening of your eyes.

The look of terror on your face
will be my ghastly song
forever then:
the retching out of notes
under eons of black skies.
Eternity is too long to sing.
Please wake, O guiltless,
guileless, unsuspecting love—
please rise.

AN EXPLANATION
OF THE AIR IMAGERY
IN GRACE BUTCHER'S POETRY

The thing about the air is,
it is as much there as things.

The feeling is of moving through air
as through water,
seeing it break
then flow together again.

At times it becomes
(for some reason—
maybe love) thicker,
and holds the shape
of the person who was in it.

The outlines, like those
in coloring books,
are almost there.

And the spaces where
certain people have been
remain
to be fallen into,
bumped into,
stumbled over,

leaned against,

also even spoken to.

Many astonishing things
hang suspended
(for some reason)
where certain people were

(maybe love).

IN NON MEMORIAM

No, I never go to see
my father and my mother—
his bones, her ashes.

The things she planted
around the house
still bloom in spring,

and his footprints
still remain under the grass
of the backyard.

I am here,
and alone.
It is my turn.

JUST CHECKING

If you asked me the difference
between being married
and how we were before,

I'd say that mainly
it's the sky being patched
so skillfully as to seem whole,

and no hysterical chicken
running around
spreading rumors.

But at night sometimes
I seem to hear scratching sounds,
and something pecks at my skull

hard, from the inside.
My thoughts turn into chicken tracks;
chaos criss-crossing in the dust;

deep in my head
the jagged edges of eggshells
scrape the backs of my eyes.

When morning comes, I'd better
take another look at the sky.

CYCLE SONG

When the roar comes
through the green summer,
it is you, coming in thunder.

I listen you along the afternoon road,
the sound in my head pulling you closer.

My eyes, closed, remember your wrists at ease
with the lightning under your hands;
the angle of your thighs eloquent,
your body speaks casual commands.

On behind you
I feel the horizons move back;
people move back and touch us
only with their eyes.

My life is at stake.
I am kept safe by the sinews
of your wrists, your fingers,
by the long hard muscles of your thighs,
by the balance that delicately moves
somewhere deep within your blood.

If there are tapestries still to be made,
one will show us with many silver threads
the color of chrome,

and the richness of the world
behind us in browns and greens.

Scarlet will mark the magic spot
where you have slain
my own invisible dragons
and carried me away.

The wild deep sound can be woven
only as golden images:
stars perhaps shattered,
falling on our shoulders;
or the sun sliding under our wheels
and lying like a deep rug
over all the land.

A MATTER OF LIFE OR DEATH

Lift up the wicked flowers
and pull down the dry stars:
the poets are dying. The big voices.
Grass breaks apart with the words
from under. I almost weep.

Here, flowers, have me. Have me, world,
flying on owlwings, flowing on
slow rivers. I have love—
if the people let me come loving.
How my skin hurts with love.
The razor of your hands
slices night into sliding sounds.
Blood may come, life may come. Who is for me?

Whose hands know first the shape of my words
before my heart drops blood through his fingers?
Wait for the forest of hands, the lake of legs.
Wait till the words of my mouth open.
Love is to take off my skin. I will. I will.
Please love my bones and my inside-out flesh.
It will be me.

The poets are dying
but grass is green in my eyes and
last night's dream fumbles at my roots.
Flowers and colors will be all sorts of roads.

"To Death," the sign says.
Yea, gladly. The poets are dying,
but my mouth fills my hand with strange shapes.
My head opens. Nothing is strange after all.
I have seen it all before. Echoes.

Through my broken pores, the surge of grass.
The poets. Their big voices. Their bodies.
Thank you. Do you hear my blood?

Let there be always a forest tangled
in the edges of all my meadows, and
knowledge of grass in the dark,
and memories pointed as stars.

The poets are dying; their hand bones crumble.
New bodies rise with the flowers.
Voices like wings of birds
scrape inside my skull, clamor in channels
of light. Death flickers. The brightness
is always the astonishing thing.